HUSTLE SMART;
NOT HARD

Maximizing Efforts for Maximum Results

ETHAN YODER

COPYRIGHT

TABLE OF CONTENTS

Delivering Great Customer Service

PUT YOURSELF IN THEIR SHOES

"There is only one boss. The customer. And he can fire everybody in the company from the chairman on down, simply by spending his money somewhere else." - Sam Walton

INTRODUCTION

As I stand at the threshold of this exploration into the realm of customer service, I'm struck by the profound significance it carries in our interconnected world. In this introductory chapter, I'll guide you through the essence of customer service, its historical evolution, and why it holds such a vital place in both the business landscape and our daily lives.

At its core, customer service is the bedrock upon which successful businesses are built. It's the art of not merely meeting customer needs but exceeding them, of not just satisfying customers but leaving them with a lasting positive impression. To grasp its importance, let's break down this definition:

- Meeting Customer Needs: This is the fundamental duty of any business. Customers come to you with needs and desires, whether it's a product they want or a problem they need solving. Customer service is the means by which you address these needs comprehensively.

- Exceeding Expectations: Good customer service is about more than just meeting baseline expectations. It's about creating a memorable experience that goes beyond what the customer anticipated. It's the smile from a barista when you order your morning coffee or the prompt and courteous response from a support agent when you encounter an issue with a product.

- Leaving a Lasting Impression: Exceptional customer service isn't just about the moment; it's about the long-lasting impact. It's the positive impression that lingers, encouraging customers to return and recommend your business to others.

The Evolution of Customer Service

To understand the significance of customer service today, we must journey through its historical evolution:

Early Days: Customer service wasn't always a structured discipline. In ancient times, it may have been as simple as a vendor remembering a loyal customer's preferences.

Then s businesses grew in scale and complexity, customer service departments emerged. These departments handled customer inquiries, complaints, and product inquiries.

In todays modern world with the advent of the internet and digital technologies revolutionized customer service. Now, customers could connect with businesses through multiple channels, from email and chat to social media.

Finally, let's delve into why great customer service matters so much in the next points.

- Customer Loyalty: Exceptional customer service fosters loyalty. When customers feel valued and well-treated, they're more likely to return to your business, even if competitors offer similar products or services.

- Positive Word-of-Mouth: Satisfied customers become brand advocates. They share their positive experiences with friends, family, and online communities, providing invaluable word-of-mouth marketing.

- Financial Success: Ultimately, great customer service impacts the bottom line. Happy customers are more likely to spend more and continue doing business with you, leading to increased revenue and profitability.

As we journey through the chapters that follow, we'll uncover the foundational principles of delivering exceptional customer service. We'll explore how to cultivate a customer-centric culture within your organization, set clear objectives, and empower your team to consistently provide outstanding service. Together, we'll unlock the secrets to not just satisfying customers but delighting them, leaving a lasting imprint that resonates far beyond the initial interaction.

CHAPTER 1:

UNDERSTANDING CUSTOMER SERVICE

As I embark on this journey to explore the fascinating world of customer service, I can't help but reflect on the profound impact it has on businesses and individuals alike. Customer service isn't just a department within an organization; it's a fundamental philosophy that can make or break a company's reputation. In this chapter, I'll delve into the core concepts of customer service, its historical evolution, and why it holds a special place in the hearts of businesses and customers worldwide.

Defining Customer Service

At its essence, customer service is the art of meeting customer needs, ensuring their satisfaction, and going above and beyond to create exceptional experiences. It encompasses all the interactions and touchpoints a customer has with a company, from the moment they first hear about a product or service to long after their purchase is made. In a world where choices abound, stellar customer service can be the differentiator that sets a business apart.

The Evolution of Customer Service

Customer service has come a long way since its inception. From the early days of face-to-face transactions at neighborhood stores to the digital age of e-commerce and chatbots, it has adapted and transformed to meet the changing needs and expectations of consumers. Understanding this evolution helps us appreciate how customer service has become not just a support function but a strategic asset for modern businesses.

The Impact of Great Customer Service

The impact of great customer service is immeasurable. It can lead to customer loyalty, positive word-of-mouth marketing, and increased revenue.

Conversely, poor customer service can result in lost customers, damaged reputations, and financial setbacks. It's not just about solving immediate issues; it's about creating lasting relationships and building trust.

In the pages that follow, we'll dive deeper into the fundamentals of great customer service, exploring the key principles that underpin its success. We'll discover how to create a customer-centric culture, set clear goals, and empower employees to deliver outstanding service. So, let's embark on this enlightening journey together as we unravel the secrets of delivering exceptional customer service and why it matters more than ever in today's competitive landscape.

All the while keep in mind Shep Hyken. Shep is a renowned customer service expert, speaker, and author known for his insights into creating exceptional customer experiences and strategies to understand and improve customer service. Shep emphasizes that great customer service goes beyond meeting customer needs; it creates loyalty, positive word-of-mouth, a competitive edge, reduced churn, a strong reputation, and enhanced profitability. It is a critical driver of business success in today's customer-centric marketplace.

"Through my extensive work in the field of customer service, I've learned that understanding customer service goes beyond simply addressing customer needs. It's about creating memorable experiences that exceed expectations and foster lasting relationships.

One fundamental lesson is that customers crave consistency. They want to know what to expect every time they interact with your business. This means maintaining consistency in the quality of service, communication, and the overall customer journey.

Another critical aspect is the power of empathy. Putting oneself in the customer's shoes and truly understanding their feelings and needs can turn an ordinary interaction into an extraordinary one. Empathy can de-escalate tense situations and create a sense of connection.

Furthermore, I've discovered that communication plays a pivotal role in customer service. Effective communication involves active listening, clear articulation, and a willingness to go the extra mile to ensure the customer fully comprehends the information. Communication is the bridge that connects businesses with their customers.

Additionally, I've seen that technology can be a valuable ally in delivering exceptional service. Leveraging modern tools, such as customer relationship management (CRM) systems and artificial intelligence (AI), can enhance efficiency and personalization. However, it's crucial to strike a balance between technology and the human touch.

Lastly, I've come to appreciate the importance of customer feedback. Customer input is a goldmine of insights that can drive improvement. Every complaint, suggestion, or praise is an opportunity to refine processes, products, and the overall customer experience.

In my experience, customer service pitfalls can manifest in various ways, and recognizing them is crucial for improving the overall customer experience. Here are some common customer service pitfalls I've observed:

- Inadequate Training: Insufficient training for customer service representatives can lead to misunderstandings, incorrect information, and frustrated customers. It's essential to invest in comprehensive training to ensure employees are well-prepared to assist customers.

- Lack of Empathy: One of the most significant pitfalls is failing to show empathy towards customers' concerns. When customers feel their emotions aren't acknowledged or understood, it can escalate tensions and dissatisfaction.

- Inconsistent Service: Inconsistency in service quality, response times, and problem resolution can erode customer trust. Customers expect a consistent experience, whether they interact with your business online, over the phone, or in person.

- Poor Communication: Communication breakdowns, such as unclear or misleading information, can frustrate customers. Effective communication is vital in conveying information accurately and managing expectations.

- Ignoring Feedback: Neglecting customer feedback and complaints is a significant pitfall. Every piece of feedback is an opportunity for improvement. Ignoring or dismissing feedback can result in repeated issues and customer churn.

- Overpromising and Underdelivering: Making promises that cannot be fulfilled is a surefire way to disappoint customers. It's better to underpromise and overdeliver to exceed expectations consistently.

- Inflexibility: An unwillingness to accommodate reasonable customer requests or adapt to unique situations can harm customer relationships. Being too rigid can deter customers from returning.

- Failing to Follow Up: After resolving an issue, it's important to follow up with the customer to ensure their satisfaction. Failing to do so leaves the customer feeling uncared for.

- Long Response Times: Delayed response times, whether in answering emails or phone calls, can lead to frustration. Prompt communication is crucial, as customers expect timely assistance.

- Ignoring Employee Feedback: Employees often have valuable insights into customer service pitfalls. Ignoring their feedback or not empowering them to suggest improvements can hinder the service quality.

- Inconsistent Policies: Policies that change frequently or are applied unevenly can lead to confusion and frustration.

Customers should know what to expect when dealing with your business.

- Lack of Ownership: Failing to take ownership of customer issues and passing them off to other departments can make customers feel unimportant and overlooked.

Recognizing these customer service pitfalls is the first step in addressing them and delivering a more exceptional customer experience. It's essential to continuously evaluate your customer service processes and make improvements based on customer feedback and changing expectations.

In summary, understanding customer service is about mastering the art of consistency, empathy, effective communication, technology integration, and leveraging customer feedback. These lessons have underscored the idea that customer service is not just a department; it's a philosophy that should permeate every aspect of a business."

CHAPTER 2:

THE FUNDAMENTALS OF

GREAT CUSTOMER SERVICE

In this chapter, we'll delve into the fundamental principles that underpin great customer service. These principles form the bedrock upon which exceptional customer experiences are built. Let's explore each of them in detail:

Building a Customer-Centric Culture

Creating a customer-centric culture is the cornerstone of great customer service. It's about instilling a mindset throughout your organization where every employee understands that satisfying and delighting customers is everyone's responsibility.

Experts like Tony Hsieh, the former CEO of Zappos, emphasized the importance of company culture in delivering outstanding service. He famously said, "Customer service shouldn't just be a department; it should be the entire company." Zappos, known for its exceptional customer service, built a culture centered on making customers happy, even if it meant going above and beyond traditional service norms.

Creating a customer-centric culture isn't just about having the words "customer first" in your mission statement. It's about instilling a mindset where every team member, from the CEO to the newest hire, understands the vital role they play in delivering exceptional service. To achieve this, consider:

- Leadership Buy-In: Leaders must champion a customer-centric mindset. When leaders demonstrate a commitment to customer service, it sets the tone for the entire organization.
- Employee Engagement: Engaged employees are more likely to embrace a customer-centric culture. Encourage open communication, listen to their ideas, and recognize their contributions.

Setting Clear Customer Service Goals

To achieve great customer service, it's essential to set clear, measurable goals. These goals serve as guideposts for your team, aligning their efforts with the overarching mission of serving customers excellently.

As customer service expert Shep Hyken notes, "Setting specific goals gives your team a sense of purpose and direction. It helps them understand what's expected and how their efforts contribute to the bigger picture." Whether it's reducing response times, increasing customer satisfaction scores, or resolving issues on the first contact, well-defined goals provide focus and motivation.

Setting clear goals in customer service provides a roadmap for your team. To make these goals effective:

- Align with Company Objectives: Ensure that your customer service goals are in sync with the overall business objectives. This alignment reinforces the importance of customer service in achieving broader success.

- Make Them Specific and Measurable: Goals should be specific, measurable, achievable, relevant, and time-bound (SMART). This clarity helps employees understand what's expected and how success will be measured.

Empowering Employees for Success

Empowered employees are the linchpin of great customer service. When employees have the autonomy to make decisions and resolve customer issues promptly, it can lead to exceptional experiences.

Richard Branson, founder of Virgin Group, is known for his emphasis on employee empowerment. He stated, "Clients do not come first. Employees come first. If you take care of your employees, they will take care of the clients." Empowered employees are more likely to take ownership of customer interactions, leading to creative problem-solving and positive outcomes.

Empowered employees are more likely to take ownership of customer interactions. To empower your team effectively:

- Training and Development: Provide ongoing training and development opportunities to equip employees with the skills and knowledge they need to excel in their roles.
- Clear Guidelines and Autonomy: Empower employees by defining clear guidelines and giving them the autonomy to make decisions within those boundaries. This shows trust in their judgment.

By understanding the nuances of building a customer-centric culture, setting clear goals, and empowering employees, you can lay a strong foundation for great customer service. These additional insights can help you navigate the challenges and complexities of implementing these fundamental principles effectively within your organization.

In this chapter, we've laid the foundation for great customer service by highlighting the importance of building a customer-centric culture, setting clear goals, and empowering employees. These principles, endorsed by experts like Tony Hsieh, Shep Hyken, and Richard Branson, provide a framework for creating a service environment that can truly distinguish your business and foster enduring customer relationships. In the upcoming chapters, we'll explore practical strategies and tactics to implement these principles effectively.

To improve your skills in understanding and implementing the fundamentals of great customer service, you can engage in various exercises and activities. Here are some exercises you can do to get better at this topic:

- Role-Playing Scenarios: Practice handling different customer service scenarios through role-playing. Enlist a colleague or friend to play the customer, and you take on the role of the customer service representative. This exercise helps you develop communication and problem-solving skills in a safe environment.

- Customer Service Feedback Analysis: Analyze customer feedback or complaints received by your organization. Try to identify common issues or trends and brainstorm solutions to address them. This exercise enhances your ability to understand customer needs and find ways to improve service.

- Mystery Shopping: Engage in mystery shopping activities where you act as a customer and evaluate the customer service of different businesses. Take note of what works well and what could be improved. This exercise provides valuable insights into real-world customer experiences.

- Customer Persona Creation: Create detailed customer personas representing different segments of your target audience. Develop empathy by putting yourself in the shoes of these fictional customers. Consider their needs, preferences, and pain points. This exercise helps you tailor your service to specific customer groups effectively.

- Customer Service Storytelling: Practice storytelling techniques to convey the importance of great customer service within your organization. Craft stories or anecdotes that highlight successful customer service experiences or lessons learned from challenging situations. Storytelling can make your message more engaging and memorable.

- Customer Service Training Modules: Design customer service training modules or materials for your team or colleagues. This exercise forces you to articulate the key principles and strategies discussed in this topic clearly. Teaching others can deepen your understanding.

- Customer Feedback Simulation: Simulate a customer feedback session. Imagine receiving feedback from a dissatisfied customer and practice responding professionally and empathetically. This exercise helps you prepare for real-life situations where handling feedback is crucial.

- Benchmarking and Best Practices Research: Research and study organizations known for their exceptional customer service. Identify best practices and strategies they employ. Implementing these practices in your own context can lead to improvements.

- Continuous Learning and Reading: Commit to ongoing learning by reading books, articles, and blogs on customer service. Engaging with industry experts and thought leaders can expand your knowledge and keep you updated on the latest trends and insights.

- Customer Service Challenges: Challenge yourself with customer service scenarios or puzzles. Set up hypothetical situations and brainstorm solutions. This exercise sharpens your problem-solving skills and encourages creativity in resolving customer issues.

Remember that improving customer service skills is an ongoing process. Consistent practice, feedback, and a commitment to learning and empathy will help you become more proficient in delivering exceptional customer service.

"Service is an attitude that resides within me. It's not just a job or a duty; it's a mindset and a commitment. It's about approaching every interaction with the intention to help and make a positive impact, whether I'm serving customers, colleagues, or the community.

This attitude involves a genuine desire to understand and fulfill the needs of others. It means actively listening, empathizing, and going the extra mile to exceed expectations. Service is not constrained by a clock; it's a continuous willingness to assist and support.

Service as an attitude is not limited to a specific role or profession. It's a way of life that influences how I engage with the world. It's about being proactive, responsive, and considerate in my actions, seeking opportunities to make a difference in the lives of others.

Ultimately, service is not just what I do; it's who I am."

I like to think that I should put myself in their shoes whenever possible.

Putting myself in someone else's shoes is an essential skill that requires empathy and understanding. Here's how I can do it in the first person:

- *Active Listening: I start by actively listening to the person I'm trying to empathize with. I pay close attention to what they are saying, without interrupting or jumping to conclusions.*
- *Ask Questions: I ask open-ended questions to gain a deeper understanding of their perspective. This helps me uncover their thoughts, feelings, and motivations.*

- *Suspend Judgment: I consciously set aside my own judgments and preconceptions. It's important not to impose my own beliefs or assumptions on their situation.*
- *Imagine Their Experience: I use my imagination to picture myself in their situation. I try to visualize what it would be like to walk in their shoes, experiencing their challenges and emotions.*
- *Express Empathy: I express empathy by acknowledging their feelings and experiences. Phrases like, "I can understand how that must feel" or "I'm here for you" convey my support and understanding.*
- *Share My Own Experiences (if relevant): If I've been in a similar situation, I might share my own experiences to create a sense of connection and show that I can relate to their feelings.*
- *Be Patient: Sometimes, it takes time for the other person to open up and share their perspective fully. I remain patient and give them the space they need to express themselves.*

- *Validate Their Emotions: I validate their emotions by letting them know that it's okay to feel the way they do. Validation can be incredibly comforting and reassuring.*
- *Offer Support: I offer my support in whatever way is appropriate. Whether it's a listening ear, assistance, or just being there for them, I let them know I'm here to help.*
- *Reflect and Learn: After the conversation, I reflect on what I've learned about their perspective and how it has deepened my understanding. This reflection helps me grow in empathy.*

Putting myself in someone else's shoes is a continuous practice of empathy and compassion. It allows me to connect with others on a deeper level, foster understanding, and build stronger relationships.

CUSTOMER SERVICE

IS <u>NOT</u> A DEPARTMENT.

It **IS AN ATTITUDE.**

~UNKNOWN

This Photo by Unknown Author is licensed under CC BY-NC-ND

CHAPTER 3:
CUSTOMER EXPECTATIONS AND NEEDS

In this chapter, we'll dive deep into the world of customer expectations and needs. Understanding what drives your customers, what they expect, and how to meet those expectations is essential for delivering exceptional service. Let's explore these crucial aspects:

Identifying Customer Expectations

To provide great customer service, we must first grasp what our customers expect from us. These expectations can vary across industries and demographics. However, some common themes emerge. Experts like Chip R. Bell, a renowned customer service author and consultant, have stressed the importance of actively seeking and understanding customer expectations. He often says, "Know what your customers want most and what your company does best. Focus on where those two meet."

Meeting Basic Customer Needs

Meeting basic customer needs is the foundation of great service. These needs often include prompt responses, clear information, and problem resolution. A failure to address these fundamental requirements can lead to dissatisfaction. As customer service expert Shep Hyken puts it, "Basic customer service is not rocket science. You just need to treat your customers as you would want to be treated."

Exceeding Customer Expectations

While meeting basic needs is essential, the true magic happens when you exceed customer expectations. This is where memorable experiences are created. Renowned marketing strategist and author Seth Godin advises, "Don't find customers for your products; find products for your customers." Going above and beyond to surprise and delight customers can turn them into loyal advocates for your brand.

While it's crucial to meet existing customer needs, exceptional service often involves anticipating future needs. This proactive approach can set you apart. As customer service expert Steve Curtin suggests in his book, "Delight Your Customers," try to predict what customers might require next, even before they realize it themselves.

The Emotional Aspect of Needs

Customers don't just have rational needs; they have emotional ones too. Understanding and addressing these emotional needs can lead to more profound connections. As Maya Angelou famously said, "People will forget what you said, people will forget what you did, but people will never forget how you made them feel." Consider how your interactions can leave customers feeling valued, heard, and cared for.

CUSTOMER
SERVICE

Cultural and Demographic Considerations

Customer needs can vary greatly based on cultural and demographic factors. What's considered exceptional service in one culture may differ from another. Take the time to learn about the diverse backgrounds and preferences of your customer base. This knowledge can help you tailor your service to resonate with different groups effectively.

Personalization and Data Analysis

In the age of data, personalization is a potent tool. By analyzing customer data and behaviors, you can customize interactions and offerings. Amazon's recommendation engine is a prime example of this. As Jeff Bezos, the company's founder, once noted, "We are not competitor-obsessed; we're customer-obsessed. We start with what the customer needs and we work backward."

Flexibility in Meeting Needs

Every customer is unique, and their needs may not always fit neatly into predefined categories. Flexibility is key. As customer service consultant Micah Solomon advises, "To provide truly great service, you must be prepared to step out of your comfort zone and meet your customer's unique needs."

Throughout this chapter, we've delved into the intricacies of customer expectations and needs, drawing on insights from experts like Chip R. Bell, Shep Hyken, and Seth Godin. Understanding what your customers want and ensuring that their basic needs are met while striving to exceed their expectations is a pivotal aspect of delivering outstanding customer service. As we progress through this book, we'll uncover strategies and techniques to effectively identify, address, and surpass these expectations, fostering strong and lasting customer relationships.

CHAPTER 4:

COMMUNICATION IN CUSTOMER SERVICE

Communication lies at the heart of exceptional customer service. In this chapter, we'll explore the art of effective communication, both verbal and non-verbal, and how it can transform customer interactions.

Effective Communication Skills

Great customer service starts with mastering effective communication skills. It's about how we convey information, listen actively, and engage with customers. As customer service expert and author Nancy Friedman advises, "The single most important skill in customer service is empathy." Empathetic communication fosters trust and understanding, essential elements in any successful interaction.

Empathy is the cornerstone of effective communication. It's not just about understanding the customer's issue but truly feeling and acknowledging their emotions. As Brené Brown, a renowned researcher and author, puts it, "Empathy has no script. There is no right way or wrong way to do it. It's simply listening, holding space, withholding judgment, emotionally connecting, and communicating that incredibly healing message of 'You're not alone.'"

Active Listening Techniques

Active listening is a skill that can make or break a customer service interaction. It involves not just hearing but fully understanding what the customer is saying. According to Stephen R. Covey, author of "The 7 Habits of Highly Effective People," "Most people do not listen with the intent to understand; they listen with the intent to reply." To excel in customer service, we must reverse this trend, focusing on understanding the customer's perspective before formulating a response.

Active listening goes beyond hearing words; it involves fully comprehending the customer's message, both spoken and unspoken. One technique is paraphrasing, where you restate what the customer has said to ensure you've understood correctly.

Another is asking open-ended questions, which encourage customers to share more details and feelings.

Dealing with Emotional Customers

Emotional customers can present unique challenges. In such situations, it's crucial to remain calm and composed. Customer service expert Richard Branson suggests, "If your staff can remain cheerful and professional under pressure, it can turn a difficult situation into a great experience."

Multichannel Communication

In today's digital age, customers interact with businesses through various channels—phone, email, chat, social media, and more. The key is to provide a consistent experience across all channels. As customer service thought leader Shep Hyken advises, "The best companies in the world deliver amazing customer service on any channel the customer wants."

Conflict Resolution Strategies

Conflict is an inevitable part of customer service. How you handle it can make or break the customer relationship. Author and mediator Kenneth Cloke suggests a problem-solving approach that involves collaborative conflict resolution, seeking mutually beneficial solutions rather than focusing on who's right or wrong.

Difficult conversations are an inevitable part of customer service. Whether it's addressing a complaint, delivering bad news, or resolving a complex issue, handling these situations with finesse is crucial. Bestselling author and communication expert Crucial Conversations: Tools for Talking When Stakes Are High," highlights the importance of dialogue in such situations. It's not just about talking but having productive, respectful conversations that lead to resolutions.

Non-Verbal Communication

Non-verbal cues, such as body language and facial expressions, play a significant role in communication.

Pay attention to your non-verbal signals, as they can convey empathy, confidence, and professionalism. Maintaining eye contact, using open body language, and offering a friendly smile can go a long way in making customers feel heard and valued.

By delving deeper into these aspects of communication in customer service, you can refine your skills and elevate your ability to create exceptional customer experiences. Empathy as a foundation, active listening techniques, handling emotional customers, mastering multichannel communication, employing conflict resolution strategies, and being mindful of non-verbal communication are all essential components of effective customer service communication.

In this chapter, we've explored the critical role of communication in customer service, drawing wisdom from experts like Nancy Friedman and Stephen R. Covey. Effective communication skills, the ability to handle difficult conversations, and active listening techniques are foundational skills for delivering exceptional customer service. As we progress through this book, we'll delve deeper into practical strategies for honing these skills and using them to create memorable customer experiences.

This Photo by Unknown Author is licensed under CC BY-SA

CHAPTER 5:

BUILDING CUSTOMER RELATIONSHIPS

In this chapter, we'll delve into the art of building and nurturing customer relationships. These relationships are the lifeblood of great customer service, and they can significantly impact a business's success. Building and nurturing customer relationships is a multifaceted endeavor that extends beyond the initial transaction. Let's delve further into this topic, exploring additional dimensions and strategies for creating strong and lasting connections with customers:

Creating Personalized Experiences

One of the most powerful ways to build customer relationships is by providing personalized experiences. As Amazon founder Jeff Bezos famously said, "We see our customers as invited guests to a party, and we are the hosts. It's our job every day to make every important aspect of the customer experience a little bit better." Tailoring your interactions and offerings to individual customer preferences fosters a sense of connection and loyalty.

Consistency is key to building trust and reliability. Customers should have a consistent experience with your brand each time they interact. As customer service expert, Ron Kaufman advises, "Consistency is not perfection. It's simply refusing to accept less than the best of which you're capable."

Personalization at Scale

In today's digital landscape, personalization is more critical than ever. Utilize data and technology to provide personalized experiences. However, it's crucial to strike a balance between personalization and privacy, ensuring customers feel comfortable with the level of personalization you offer.

Proactive Outreach

Don't wait for customers to reach out with concerns or issues. Proactively reach out to check on their satisfaction, offer assistance, or provide relevant information. This proactive approach can demonstrate your commitment to their well-being and needs.

Customer Loyalty and Retention

Loyal customers are not just repeat buyers; they are brand advocates who sing your praises to others. According to Frederick F. Reichheld, author of "The Loyalty Effect," "The only path to profitable growth may lie in a company's ability to get its loyal customers to become, in effect, its marketing department." Building strong customer relationships is the key to fostering this loyalty and retaining valuable customers over the long term.

Loyalty Programs

Implementing a well-designed loyalty program can incentivize repeat business and reward loyal customers. However, it's essential to make these programs genuinely valuable and not just gimmicks. As Fred Reichheld, author of "The Loyalty Effect," suggests, "Loyalty programs that are truly loyalty-enhancing don't require complex point schemes, just a simple promise to 'make your life easier.'"

Managing Customer Feedback

Feedback is a precious resource in building customer relationships. It provides insights into what's working well and where improvements are needed. As Bill Gates, co-founder of Microsoft, observed, "Your most unhappy customers are your greatest source of learning." Actively seeking and responding to customer feedback not only improves your products or services but also demonstrates that you value your customers' opinions.

Gathering and Utilizing Customer Feedback

Regularly seek feedback from customers about their experiences with your brand. Analyze this feedback to identify areas for improvement. Customers appreciate when they see their input resulting in positive changes.

Community Building

Foster a sense of community around your brand. Create platforms where customers can interact with each other, share their experiences, and offer peer-to-peer support. This sense of belonging can deepen their connection to your brand.

By exploring these additional dimensions of building customer relationships, you can refine your strategies for creating strong, enduring, and mutually beneficial connections with your customers. Consistency in service, personalization at scale, proactive outreach, loyalty programs, gathering and utilizing customer feedback, and community building are all valuable components of effective relationship-building in customer service.

CUSTOMER RELATIONSHIP MANAGEMENT

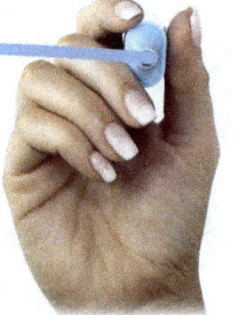

Here's a quote from Paul Greenberg, a well-known expert on customer relationship management (CRM):

"CRM is not about a one-time transaction. It's about building relationships one interaction at a time." - Paul Greenberg

This quote underscores the core principle of CRM, which is to foster and nurture long-term relationships with customers through ongoing, meaningful interactions and engagement.

To be sure and instill in the importance of this topic I want to present to you an example of a company that in my opinion does this very well.

One company that truly excels in building customer relationships, in my view, is Amazon. Here's how Amazon demonstrates its commitment to customer relationships:

Personalized Recommendations: Amazon uses advanced algorithms to offer personalized product recommendations based on my browsing and purchase history. This not only makes my shopping experience convenient but also shows that they understand my preferences.

Customer Reviews and Ratings: Amazon provides a platform for customers to leave reviews and ratings for products. This transparency allows me to make informed decisions and feel like part of a community of shoppers.

Amazon Prime: The Amazon Prime program offers various benefits, including fast shipping, exclusive deals, and access to streaming content. It's a prime example (pun intended) of how Amazon invests in retaining and rewarding loyal customers.

Efficient Customer Support: Amazon's customer support is known for its efficiency. If I have an issue with an order, their responsive customer service team is quick to address it, often with hassle-free returns or replacements.

Customer-Centric Policies: Amazon's return policy is customer-friendly, and they stand behind their products. Knowing that I can return items with ease gives me confidence in my purchases.

Amazon Web Services (AWS): Even in the B2B space, Amazon has built strong customer relationships through AWS. Many companies rely on AWS for cloud services, and Amazon's commitment to service excellence is evident in their robust infrastructure and support.

Innovation and Convenience: Amazon continually innovates to enhance the convenience of shopping. Initiatives like Amazon Go stores and voice-activated shopping with Alexa show their dedication to improving the customer experience.

Community Engagement: Amazon engages with its customers through community forums and discussion boards. It's a place where I can seek advice, share experiences, and connect with fellow Amazon users.

Amazon Smile: The Amazon Smile program allows me to support charitable organizations while shopping. This demonstrates Amazon's commitment not only to customers but also to broader social causes.

Prime Video and Kindle: Amazon's Prime Video and Kindle platforms offer additional value to Prime members. These services create a more holistic customer experience and strengthen the Amazon ecosystem.

Amazon's relentless focus on customer-centricity, convenience, and innovation has played a significant role in building and maintaining strong customer relationships. Their ability to adapt to evolving customer needs and preferences is a testament to their commitment to customer satisfaction.

CHAPTER 6:

TECHNOLOGY AND CUSTOMER SERVICE

In today's digital age, technology plays a pivotal role in shaping customer service. This chapter delves into the symbiotic relationship between technology and exceptional customer service.

Leveraging Technology for Enhanced Service

Modern technology offers a plethora of tools to enhance customer service. As I've learned from the insights of Micah Solomon, a renowned customer service consultant and author, "Technology should be an enabler, not a barrier, to great customer service." It can streamline processes, automate routine tasks, and provide valuable data to better understand and serve customers.

Automation vs. Personalization

Automation is a double-edged sword in customer service. On one hand, it can increase efficiency and reduce response times. On the other hand, it risks depersonalizing interactions. Striking the right balance between automation and personalization is crucial. As customer experience expert Blake Morgan emphasizes, "Customers still want the human touch, even in a digital age." Using technology to enhance personalization rather than replace it can create exceptional customer experiences.

Integrating Customer Service Channels

Customers now interact with businesses through various channels, from email and phone to social media and chat. Effective omnichannel customer service is about ensuring a consistent and seamless experience across all touchpoints. As customer service thought leader Shep Hyken advises,

"The best companies in the world deliver amazing customer service on any channel the customer wants."

Omnichannel Customer Support

In our digital age, customers expect to interact with businesses seamlessly across various channels, from phone and email to social media and chat. Implementing an effective omnichannel strategy ensures that customers receive consistent service, regardless of how they reach out. However, it's vital to integrate these channels seamlessly to provide a unified experience.

Artificial Intelligence (AI) and Chatbots

AI-powered chatbots are becoming increasingly prevalent in customer service. These virtual assistants can handle routine inquiries and tasks, freeing up human agents for more complex issues. However, it's essential to strike a balance, as customers still value human interaction. As Andrew Ng, a prominent AI researcher, advises, "Just as electricity transformed almost everything 100 years ago, today I actually have a hard time thinking of an industry that I don't think AI will transform in the next several years."

Data Analytics and Personalization

Data analytics enables businesses to gain deeper insights into customer behavior and preferences. By harnessing this data, you can personalize interactions and recommendations. Remember, though, that with great power comes great responsibility. Safeguarding customer data and respecting privacy are paramount.

Self-Service Portals

Many customers prefer self-service options for quick problem resolution. Develop user-friendly self-service portals and knowledge bases to empower customers to find answers independently. As Salesforce CEO Marc Benioff notes, "The business of business is improving the state of the world."

Automation and Efficiency

Automation tools can streamline processes, reducing response times and improving efficiency. However, use automation judiciously. As Bill Gates once said, "The first rule of any technology used in a business is that automation applied to an efficient operation will magnify the efficiency. The second is that automation applied to an inefficient operation will magnify the inefficiency."

Data Security and Trust

In an era of data breaches and privacy concerns, customer trust is paramount. Implement robust security measures to protect customer data. Trust is hard-won and easily lost, as indicated by the adage, "Trust arrives on foot but leaves on horseback."

By considering these additional dimensions of technology's role in customer service, you can harness its potential effectively while navigating the challenges it presents. Omnichannel support, AI and chatbots, data analytics, self-service portals, automation, and data security and trust are all critical aspects of delivering exceptional customer service in our tech-driven world.

I wanted to showcase a company that does this topic very well in my opinion and that is Apple.

Here's how Apple leverages technology to enhance the customer experience:

- *Apple Support App: Apple offers an Apple Support app that provides quick access to product information, troubleshooting guides, and the ability to schedule appointments at Apple Stores or with Apple's online support.*

- *Live Chat Support: Apple provides a live chat option on its website and within the Apple Support app. This enables customers to chat with*

Apple representatives in real time, seeking assistance and solutions to their issues.

- *AppleCare: AppleCare is a suite of customer support services that includes phone support, live chat, and the ability to schedule service appointments. It extends beyond the standard warranty, offering peace of mind to customers.*

- *Apple Communities: Apple hosts online community forums where customers can ask questions, share experiences, and seek advice from fellow Apple users. It's a valuable resource for troubleshooting and getting insights from the community.*

- *Remote Diagnostics: Apple uses technology for remote diagnostics and troubleshooting. Apple support representatives can remotely access and diagnose issues with customers' devices, often resolving them without the need for a physical visit.*

- *Apple Store Appointments: Customers can schedule appointments at Apple Stores using the Apple Store app. This ensures that they receive personalized assistance and reduces wait times.*

- *AppleCare Website Resources: Apple's website is rich in resources, including articles, videos, and user guides, that help customers troubleshoot issues on their own.*

- *Online Orders and Tracking: Apple's website and app allow customers to track their orders, making it easy to monitor the progress of product deliveries.*

- *Apple Support on Social Media: Apple has an active presence on social media platforms, providing support and updates to customers through channels like Twitter and Facebook.*

Apple Wallet Integration: Apple integrates support-related information, such as warranty details and service appointments, into the Apple Wallet app for easy access.

Apple's seamless integration of technology into its customer service ecosystem enhances convenience, accessibility, and the overall customer experience. Whether it's through online resources, live chat support, remote diagnostics, or appointment scheduling, Apple leverages technology to make customer interactions more efficient and effective.

In this chapter, we've explored the dynamic relationship between technology and customer service, drawing wisdom from experts like Micah Solomon, Blake Morgan, and Shep Hyken. Leveraging technology for enhanced service, finding the right balance between automation and personalization, and seamlessly integrating customer service channels are all critical aspects of delivering outstanding customer experiences in the digital age. As we proceed through this book, we'll uncover practical strategies to harness technology's potential for the benefit of both businesses and customers.

CHAPTER 7:

TRAINING AND DEVELOPMENT

In this chapter, we'll explore the critical role of training and development in creating a team that excels in delivering great customer service. Effective training programs can empower employees, enhance their skills, and foster a customer-centric mindset.

Ron Kaufman, an expert in customer service shares his perspective below.

"Creating an exceptional service culture is not just a goal; it's a fundamental necessity for any organization that seeks long-term success. In my years of working with companies around the world, I've observed that the most successful ones prioritize service excellence at every level.

To foster an exceptional service culture, it begins with leadership. Leaders must champion the cause of service and set the tone for the entire organization. They should lead by example, demonstrating a commitment to service excellence in their actions and decisions.

Furthermore, it's crucial to make service a shared responsibility. Every team member, regardless of their role, plays a vital part in delivering exceptional service. From the frontline staff who interact directly with customers to those working behind the scenes, everyone should understand the significance of their contributions to the customer experience.

Training and development are integral components of this journey. Investing in training ensures that employees have the skills, knowledge, and tools needed to provide outstanding service. Continuous learning and development programs keep the team updated on evolving customer needs and industry trends.

Moreover, feedback mechanisms are essential. Encourage open communication channels where employees can share their insights and concerns. Customer feedback should be analyzed regularly, and improvements should be implemented based on these insights.

Training Frontline Staff

Frontline staff are the face of your organization, and their interactions with customers are pivotal. As renowned customer service consultant and author Shep Hyken aptly puts it, "Your frontline employees are your company's first line of defense. They're responsible for delivering exceptional service and representing your brand." Investing in their training ensures they are well-prepared to handle diverse customer interactions.

Continuous Learning and Improvement

Learning doesn't end with initial training. Continuous learning is vital for staying updated on evolving customer expectations, technologies, and industry trends. As customer service expert, Nancy Friedman states, "The best customer service training is ongoing. It's the reinforcement of good habits and best practices over time that makes a difference."

Building a Customer-Centric Team

Creating a customer-centric team requires more than just training; it's about instilling a mindset that prioritizes customer satisfaction. As Howard Schultz, former CEO of Starbucks, once said, "We're not in the coffee business serving people, but in the people business serving coffee." This customer-centric approach should permeate every aspect of your team's culture and operations.

Training and development are essential to providing great customer service for several compelling reasons:

- Skill Enhancement: Effective customer service requires a specific set of skills, including active listening, problem-solving, empathy, and effective communication. Training programs help employees develop and refine these skills, ensuring they can handle customer interactions with competence and professionalism.

- Consistency: Training programs establish consistent standards and practices for customer service. When all employees receive the same training, customers can expect a uniform level of service quality, regardless of who they interact with. This consistency builds trust and reliability.

- Product Knowledge: Customer service representatives must have in-depth knowledge of the products or services they are supporting. Training equips employees with the information they need to answer customer questions accurately and resolve issues efficiently.

- Confidence: Adequate training boosts employees' confidence in their ability to handle customer inquiries and resolve problems. Confident employees are more likely to engage positively with customers and provide solutions that meet their needs.

- Adaptation to Change: The business environment is dynamic, and customer expectations can change rapidly. Ongoing training ensures that employees stay up-to-date with evolving customer needs, technologies, and industry trends, enabling them to adapt and respond effectively.

- Problem Resolution: Training programs often include scenarios and simulations that mimic real-world customer interactions. This prepares employees to handle a wide range of customer issues and complaints, improving their problem-solving abilities.

- Cultural Alignment: Training can also reinforce the organization's culture, emphasizing the importance of customer-centric values and principles. When employees are aligned with these values, they are more likely to prioritize customer satisfaction.

- Employee Engagement and Satisfaction: Providing opportunities for training and development can boost employee morale and job satisfaction. Employees who feel supported in their professional growth are more likely to be motivated and engaged in delivering exceptional service.

- Retention and Promotion: Companies that invest in employee training and development often experience higher employee retention rates. Additionally, well-trained employees are more likely to be considered for promotions and leadership roles within the organization, further benefiting the customer service team.

- Competitive Advantage: Exceptional customer service can be a significant differentiator in a competitive market. Well-trained employees are better equipped to provide outstanding service, which can lead to customer loyalty and a competitive edge.

In summary, training and development are critical because they equip employees with the knowledge, skills, and confidence needed to provide exceptional customer service. They ensure consistency, adaptability, and alignment with organizational values, leading to improved customer satisfaction and a competitive advantage in the marketplace.

In this chapter, we've explored the significance of training and development in delivering exceptional customer service, drawing insights from experts like Shep Hyken, Nancy Friedman, and Howard Schultz. Training frontline staff, promoting continuous learning, and fostering a customer-centric team culture are essential steps towards building a team that consistently delights customers. As we proceed through this book, we'll uncover actionable strategies to design effective training programs and nurture a customer-focused workforce.

CHAPTER 8:

HANDLING CUSTOMER COMPLAINTS

AND DIFFICULT SITUATIONS

In this chapter, we'll explore the art of handling customer complaints and navigating challenging situations. It's a crucial aspect of customer service, as how you deal with issues can significantly impact customer satisfaction and loyalty.

Dealing with Irate Customers

Irate customers can be a formidable challenge. However, as American author and motivational speaker Zig Ziglar wisely noted, "Every sale has five basic obstacles: no need, no money, no hurry, no desire, no trust." When customers are upset, it often comes down to trust. Calmly addressing their concerns and resolving issues can rebuild that trust.

Turning Complaints into Opportunities

Complaints are not merely problems to solve; they are opportunities to demonstrate your commitment to customer satisfaction. The renowned customer service expert Ron Kaufman encapsulates this idea by saying, "Every service challenge is an opportunity to recover customer loyalty, even if the customer doesn't yet know it." Turning a negative experience into a positive one can create loyal customers who appreciate your dedication to their needs.

Conflict Resolution Techniques

Conflict resolution is a valuable skill in customer service. It's about finding mutually satisfactory solutions to disputes. As Kenneth Thomas, an expert in conflict resolution, explains, "Conflict is inevitable, but combat is optional." Employing effective conflict resolution techniques can help resolve issues amicably, preserving the customer's relationship with your business.

here are methods from two experts on how to handle customer complaints:

Ron Kaufman's Service Recovery Method:

Expert: Ron Kaufman is a renowned customer service consultant and author.

Method: Ron Kaufman emphasizes a proactive approach to service recovery. His method involves listening to the customer's complaint attentively, empathizing with their situation, apologizing sincerely, and taking immediate action to resolve the issue. He believes in going above and beyond to not only resolve the problem but to turn the negative experience into a positive one, thereby winning back the customer's trust and loyalty.

Micah Solomon's Empathetic Listening Method:

Expert: Micah Solomon is a customer service consultant and author.

Method: Micah Solomon advocates for empathetic listening when handling customer complaints. His method involves actively listening to the customer's concerns without interrupting, acknowledging their emotions, and using phrases that convey understanding and empathy. This approach helps customers feel heard and valued, paving the way for a more productive and positive resolution to the complaint.

Both of these methods prioritize empathy, active listening, and immediate action in addressing customer complaints, with the ultimate goal of turning dissatisfied customers into loyal advocates.

While you never know how you are going to handle one of these situations it may be a good idea to do a role play exercise to have an idea of what may occur.

Role-Playing Exercise: Handling a Customer Complaint

This role-playing exercise is designed to help you practice handling a customer complaint effectively. It can be done individually or in a group setting.

Scenario:

You are a customer who purchased a faulty product from an electronics store. You are frustrated and want a resolution.

Instructions:

Set the Scene: One participant (the Customer) takes on the role of a frustrated customer, and the other participant (the Customer Service Representative) takes on the role of the company's representative.

Act Out the Scenario: The Customer initiates the conversation by expressing their complaint about the faulty product. They should be emotional and frustrated in their approach.

Customer Service Representative's Role: The Customer Service Representative's goal is to defuse the situation, address the complaint, and find a resolution. Use active listening, empathy, and problem-solving skills to guide the conversation.

Customer's Role: The Customer's role is to express their frustration, provide details about the issue, and be vocal about their expectations for a resolution.

Practice Key Techniques:

Active Listening: The Customer Service Representative should actively listen to the customer's complaint without interrupting.

Empathy: Show empathy by acknowledging the customer's frustration and emotions.

Apologize: Offer a sincere apology for the inconvenience caused.

Problem-Solving: Work with the customer to find a suitable resolution, such as a refund, replacement, or repair.

Follow-Up: Ensure the customer is satisfied with the proposed solution and ask if they have any additional concerns.

Feedback and Reflection:

After the role-play, both participants should provide feedback on each other's performance.

Discuss what went well and what could be improved.

Reflect on the experience and consider how the techniques used could be applied in real-life customer service interactions.

Switch Roles: If working in a group, switch roles and repeat the exercise, allowing everyone to practice both sides of the interaction.

This role-playing exercise helps participants develop their customer service skills, especially in handling difficult and emotional customer complaints. It provides an opportunity to practice active listening, empathy, problem-solving, and conflict resolution techniques in a controlled setting, preparing individuals for real-life customer interactions.

I would like to be sure I stress the importance of this topic.

The price of not handling complaints well is something I've witnessed firsthand, and it can be quite steep. Here's how I perceive the consequences of mishandling complaints:

- Customer Churn: When complaints aren't addressed satisfactorily, customers are more likely to take their business elsewhere. This loss of customer loyalty can have a significant impact on revenue and growth.

- Negative Word-of-Mouth: Unhappy customers often share their bad experiences with friends, family, and on social media. Negative word-of-mouth can tarnish a company's reputation and deter potential customers.

- Damage to Brand Image: A reputation for poor complaint handling can damage a brand's image and erode trust. It may take a long time to rebuild that trust once it's lost.

- Reduced Customer Lifetime Value: Mishandling complaints can shorten the lifetime value of a customer. When customers have a negative experience, they're less likely to make repeat purchases or become brand advocates.

- Missed Improvement Opportunities: Customer complaints can be valuable sources of feedback for improvement. Failing to address complaints means missing out on insights that could lead to better products, services, or processes.

- Legal and Regulatory Issues: Depending on the nature of the complaint, there may be legal or regulatory consequences for not addressing it properly. This can lead to fines, legal disputes, or damage to a company's standing.

- Employee Disengagement: Poor complaint handling can also affect employee morale. If employees witness customer dissatisfaction and feel powerless to resolve issues, they may become disengaged or frustrated.

- Resource Drain: Mishandling complaints can lead to an unnecessary drain on resources. It often requires more time, effort, and resources to deal with escalated complaints or address recurring issues.

- Missed Growth Opportunities: Satisfied customers are more likely to refer others and contribute to a company's growth. Mishandling complaints can hinder organic growth through referrals.

- Competitive Disadvantage: Companies that consistently fail to handle complaints well put themselves at a competitive disadvantage. Competitors with superior customer service are more likely to capture market share.

In summary, not handling complaints effectively can result in financial losses, reputational damage, legal issues, and missed opportunities for growth. It's a costly oversight that can impact a company's long-term success and sustainability.

Because of this I would like to showcase an example of a company that does this very well.

Here's how Nordstrom excels in addressing customer complaints:

Responsive Customer Service: Nordstrom's customer service team is highly responsive. They acknowledge customer complaints promptly and ensure that the issue is addressed without delay.

Empathetic Approach: Nordstrom's customer service representatives show empathy and understanding when dealing with complaints. They listen actively to customers' concerns and express genuine care.

Flexibility in Returns and Exchanges: Nordstrom is known for its generous return and exchange policy. They make it easy for customers to return or exchange products, even if the issue is not due to a manufacturing defect.

Effective Problem Resolution: Nordstrom focuses on resolving complaints effectively and to the customer's satisfaction. They are empowered to make decisions and provide solutions that prioritize the customer's needs.

Personalized Follow-Up: After resolving a complaint, Nordstrom often follows up with the customer to ensure their satisfaction. This personalized touch demonstrates a commitment to long-term customer relationships.

Feedback Utilization: Nordstrom values customer feedback and uses it to drive improvements. They actively seek feedback and make adjustments to enhance the overall customer experience.

Employee Training: Nordstrom invests in extensive employee training to equip them with the skills and knowledge needed to handle customer complaints professionally and effectively.

Consistency: Nordstrom maintains a high level of consistency in its customer service approach, ensuring that customers receive a similar level of care and attention across all locations and touchpoints.

Transparency: Nordstrom is transparent in its communication with customers. If there are delays or issues, they proactively inform customers and provide updates on the resolution process.

Online and In-Store Support: Nordstrom offers customer support through various channels, including in-store assistance, online chat, phone support, and email. This multi-channel approach ensures customers can choose their preferred method of communication.

Nordstrom's customer-centric approach and commitment to resolving complaints swiftly and effectively contribute to its reputation for outstanding customer service. Their emphasis on empathy, flexibility, and continuous improvement makes them a prime example of a company that excels in handling customer complaints.

CHAPTER9:
MONITORING AND LOGGING

In this chapter, we'll explore the critical process of measuring and continuously improving customer service. It's essential to have metrics in place to gauge your performance and identify areas where enhancements are needed.

Key Performance Indicators (KPIs)

Measuring customer service effectiveness begins with defining key performance indicators (KPIs). These are specific metrics that align with your customer service goals. As customer experience strategist Jeanne Bliss emphasizes, "What gets measured gets managed." KPIs provide quantifiable insights into how well your team is meeting customer needs.

Customer Satisfaction Surveys

Customer satisfaction surveys are invaluable tools for gauging how customers perceive your service. As customer service expert Micah Solomon advises, "Use surveys to gather feedback and insights directly from your customers. Their opinions are gold." These surveys can reveal areas of strength and opportunities for improvement, helping you tailor your service to customer preferences.

Implementing Service Improvements

Customer feedback, KPIs, and survey data are only valuable if they lead to action. As business management expert Peter Drucker famously stated, "What gets measured gets improved." Analyzing the information you gather and using it to drive improvements is a continuous process. It may involve refining processes, enhancing training programs, or implementing new technologies to better serve your customers.

Let's delve deeper into the realm of measuring and improving customer service, exploring additional dimensions and strategies to ensure excellence in this critical aspect of business:

Customer Feedback Analysis

Analyzing customer feedback is a goldmine for insights. Beyond simply collecting feedback, understanding how to interpret and act upon it is crucial. Whether it's through surveys, reviews, or direct customer interactions, every piece of feedback can provide valuable information about what's working and where improvements are needed.

Service Recovery Strategies

Even with the best intentions, sometimes things go wrong. Service recovery strategies are essential for turning negative experiences into positive ones. These strategies involve swift action to address a customer's concern, offering compensation when appropriate, and ensuring that the customer leaves with a positive impression of how the issue was resolved.

Benchmarking Against Industry Standards

To gauge the effectiveness of your customer service, it's beneficial to benchmark your performance against industry standards and competitors. This comparative analysis can reveal areas where you excel and areas where you may be falling short. Remember, excellence in customer service often means striving to surpass industry norms.

Employee Feedback and Engagement

Employee satisfaction and engagement are intrinsically tied to the quality of customer service. Employees who are content and engaged tend to deliver better service. Therefore, it's essential to solicit and act upon employee feedback, ensuring they have the tools, resources, and support needed to provide excellent service.

Service Recovery Costs vs. Customer Retention

Balancing the cost of service recovery with customer retention is a delicate equation. Harvard Business Review's research has shown that it's often more cost-effective to retain a customer through effective service recovery than to acquire new customers. Understanding this balance can guide investment decisions in customer service.

Leveraging Technology for Measurement

In today's data-driven world, technology plays a vital role in measuring and improving customer service. Customer relationship management (CRM) systems, data analytics, and artificial intelligence can provide valuable insights and automation opportunities. However, it's crucial to use technology as an enabler of human connection, not a replacement for it.

By exploring these additional dimensions of measuring and improving customer service, you can refine your strategies and tactics for delivering exceptional experiences to your customers. Effective feedback analysis, service recovery, benchmarking, employee engagement, cost considerations, and leveraging technology are all essential components of a comprehensive approach to elevating your customer service standards.

In this chapter, we've explored the importance of measuring and improving customer service, drawing insights from experts like Jeanne Bliss, Micah Solomon, and Peter Drucker. Establishing KPIs, conducting customer satisfaction surveys, and implementing service improvements are essential steps in ensuring that your customer service efforts remain aligned with customer expectations and business goals. As we proceed in this book, we'll delve deeper into specific strategies and tactics for measuring, analyzing, and enhancing your customer service performance.

CHAPTER 10:
CASE STUDIES IN GREAT CUSTOMER SERVICE

In this chapter, we'll explore real-world case studies that exemplify outstanding customer service. Learning from these success stories can provide valuable insights and inspiration for your own customer service journey.

Real-World Examples of Exceptional Service

One of the best ways to understand and implement great customer service is by examining how successful businesses have achieved it. As bestselling author and customer service expert Shep Hyken often emphasizes, "The magic of amazing customer service isn't a secret; it's in plain sight." By examining these case studies, we can uncover the strategies and practices that have propelled these businesses to excellence.

Learning from Success Stories

Studying success stories in customer service can offer numerous takeaways:

Disney's Legendary Customer Experience: Disney's commitment to creating magical experiences for its guests is renowned. The Disney Institute, a division of The Walt Disney Company, shares valuable insights into its customer-centric approach. As they say, "Remember, creating a great guest experience isn't magic; it's method."

Zappos' Exceptional Customer Loyalty: Zappos, an online shoe and clothing retailer, is celebrated for its customer service. The company's founder, Tony Hsieh, emphasized the importance of a strong company culture. He said, "Our number one priority is company culture. Our whole belief is that if you get the culture right, most of the other stuff, like delivering great customer service or building a long-term enduring brand, will just happen naturally."

Ritz-Carlton's Legendary Service: The Ritz-Carlton Hotel Company is known for its unwavering commitment to service excellence. Their credo, the "Gold Standards," outlines the principles that guide their customer service efforts. As Horst Schulze, one of the founders of Ritz-Carlton, noted, "The answer is yes; what is the question?" This mentality reflects their dedication to meeting customer needs.

They do this so well in fact that The Ritz-Carlton is renowned for its exceptional customer service, and their Gold Standards principles are the foundation of this service philosophy. These principles guide every aspect of the Ritz-Carlton's operations and interactions with guests. Here are the key elements of the Ritz-Carlton Gold Standards:

The Ritz-Carlton's Gold Standards begin with a Credo, a statement of their commitment to providing the finest personal service and facilities. This Credo sets the tone for the entire organization, emphasizing the importance of exceeding customer expectations.

The Three Steps of Service:

1. A Warm and Sincere Greeting: The first step is a warm and sincere greeting. Team members are trained to use the guest's name (if known) and make eye contact to create a personal connection.

2. Anticipation and Fulfillment of Guest Needs: The second step involves anticipating and fulfilling guest needs. Team members are encouraged to anticipate what the guest may require and offer assistance proactively.

3. Fond Farewell: The third step is a fond farewell. This involves expressing appreciation for the guest's business and ensuring their departure is as pleasant as their arrival.

The 12 Service Values:

- I Am Proud to Be Ritz-Carlton
- I Build Strong Relationships and Create Ritz-Carlton Guests for Life
- I Am Always Responsive to the Expressions of Our Guests
- I Am Empowered to Create Unique, Memorable, and Personal Experiences for Our Guests
- I Am Here to Serve
- I Am Involved in the Continuous Pursuit of Excellence
- I Am Committed to the Spirit to Serve Philosophy
- I Am Responsible for the Guest's Experience
- I Seek Opportunities to Innovate and Improve the Ritz-Carlton Experience
- I Own and Immediately Resolve Guest Problems
- I Create a Work Environment of Respect and Support for All Team Members
- I Am Involved in the Planning of the Work That Affects Me

They have the following Motto

"We are Ladies and Gentlemen serving Ladies and Gentlemen." This motto emphasizes the respectful and courteous treatment of both guests and employees.

These are the fundamental behaviors expected from all employees. They include smiling, making eye contact, offering a warm and sincere greeting, listening, and responding promptly and professionally.

These values guide employees in their interactions with guests and each other. They include respecting and caring for guests and each other, taking pride in their work, and being empowered to create memorable experiences.

The Ritz-Carlton makes a promise to its employees: "At The Ritz-Carlton, our Ladies and Gentlemen are the most important resource in our service commitment to our guests." This promise underscores the importance of valuing and nurturing their employees.

Employees are encouraged to create "WOW" moments for guests—those unforgettable experiences that go beyond expectations and leave a lasting impression.

The Ritz-Carlton is committed to continuous improvement. They gather and analyze guest feedback to identify areas for enhancement and consistently strive to raise the bar on service excellence.

These Gold Standards are deeply ingrained in the Ritz-Carlton culture and represent a commitment to providing world-class customer service. They serve as a blueprint for delivering exceptional experiences to every guest, ensuring that each visit to a Ritz-Carlton property is memorable and unforgettable.

Summary

In this chapter, we've explored case studies of businesses renowned for their exceptional customer service, drawing wisdom from experts like Shep Hyken, The Disney Institute, Tony Hsieh, and Horst Schulze. Learning from these success stories allows us to extract valuable lessons and strategies that can be applied to our own customer service endeavors. As we proceed through this book, we'll use these insights to shape our approach to delivering outstanding customer service.

In conclusion, " Delivering Great Customer Service " is a call to action. It urges all of us to embrace the mindset to put ourselves in their shoes, to recognizing that the journey of self-improvement is ongoing. As the world evolves, so must our ability to deliver greater customer service. Through this exploration, my goal was to inspire readers to cultivate a holistic skill set that positions them not just as experts in their fields but as adept navigators of the complex, interconnected tapestry of human relationships.

Kindest regards

Noe Tovar

SCAN FOR AUTHOR PAGE TO ACCESS
OTHER BOOKS BY THIS AUTHOR

WRITER'S NOTE

As the author of this book on customer service, I want to express my sincere appreciation for taking the time to explore the various facets of providing exceptional service to your customers. This book has been a labor of love, drawing upon my own experiences and the invaluable insights shared by experts in the field.

In today's competitive business landscape, customer service is not merely a necessity; it is a strategic imperative. The way we engage with our customers shapes their perceptions, influences their loyalty, and ultimately defines our success. Through these chapters, I've endeavored to provide you with a comprehensive guide that goes beyond the basics, offering in-depth perspectives and practical strategies to elevate your customer service efforts.

Whether you're a seasoned professional seeking to refine your approach or someone new to the world of customer service, I hope this book serves as a valuable resource. It's not just a manual of best practices; it's an exploration of the art and science of delivering outstanding customer experiences.

I encourage you to approach each chapter with an open mind and a commitment to continuous improvement. As you navigate the complexities of customer expectations, communication, technology, and more, remember that exceptional customer service is not a destination but a journey. It's about consistently striving to exceed customer needs, embracing feedback as a catalyst for growth, and fostering a culture where every team member understands the significance of their role in creating lasting customer relationships.

I would like to express my gratitude to the experts and thought leaders whose wisdom has enriched these pages, and to you, the reader, for your dedication to delivering exceptional customer service. May the insights shared within these chapters empower you to not only meet but exceed your customers' expectations, ultimately leading to stronger, more enduring relationships and business success.

Wishing you an inspiring and transformative journey in your pursuit of great customer service.

Warm regards,